My Country
Ukraine

Annabel Savery

W
FRANKLIN WATTS
LONDON•SYDNEY

First published in 2012
by Franklin Watts

Copyright © Franklin Watts 2012

Franklin Watts
338 Euston Road
London NW1 3BH

Franklin Watts Australia
Level 17/207 Kent Street
Sydney, NSW 2000

All rights reserved.

Dewey number: 947.7'0863
ISBN: 978 1 4451 1050 9

Printed in China

Series Editor: Paul Rockett
Series Designer: Paul Cherrill
    for Basement68
Picture Researcher: Diana Morris

Franklin Watts is a division of
Hachette Children's Books,
an Hachette UK company.

www.hachette.co.uk

Every attempt has been made to clear copyright.
Should there be any inadvertent omission please apply
to the publisher for rectification.

Picture credits: Slav Bukhai/Shutterstock: 10; Stephen Coyne/Art
Directors/Alamy: 13c; Dmitro2009/Shutterstock: front cover l;
Sergii Figurnyl/Shutterstock: front cover c, 4c, 9b, 13b, 16b, 18b, 22t;
Anton Gvozdikov/Shutterstock: 2, 19; Hamsterman/Shutterstock:
14; Ferdinand Hollweek/Alamy: 9c; Idealink Photography/Alamy: 16c;
Thomas Imo/Alamy: 17; joyfull/Shutterstock: 7; Yana Kabagbu/
Shutterstock: 15t; Sergey Kamshylin/Shutterstock: front cover r, 11;
Oleksandr Kotenko/Shutterstock: 8; Alexandra Lande/Shutterstock:
5; mycola/Shutterstock: 6; Oleg Nikishin/Getty Images: 15b; Olinchuk/
Shutterstock: 4bl; Dmitri Ometsinsky /Shutterstock: 20; pdesign/
Shutterstock: 22c; Elena Pollshchuk/Shutterstock: 18c; Gennadiy
Poznyakov/Alamy: 1, 12; Kostyantyn Sulima/Shutterstock: 24;
Lilyana Vynogradova/Alamy: 21.

Contents

All words in **bold** appear in the glossary on page 23.

Ukraine in the world

My name is Anatoliy and I live in Ukraine.

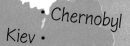

• Chernobyl
Kiev •

Dnipropetrovsk •

• Odesa

Ukraine's place in the world.

I live in Dnipropetrovsk (say 'dnee-proh-peh-trov-szk'), which is a city in the east of Ukraine.

Ukraine is in the continent of Europe. After Russia, Ukraine is the biggest country in Europe.

Many countries border Ukraine. These include Belarus, Russia, Poland, Slovakia, Hungary, Romania and Moldova.

This is Kiev, the capital city of Ukraine.

Ukraine's landscape

This machine is used for harvesting crops.

Much of the land in Ukraine is open **steppe**. This is flat grassland where farmers can raise animals.

The soil is rich and **fertile**, which means it is very good for growing crops, such as **cereals** and vegetables. There are also large areas covered by thick forest.

In 1986, there was a disaster at Chernobyl, a **nuclear power plant** in the north of Ukraine.

The disaster has left the ground around the site **contaminated** by **radioactive** material.

This is the nuclear power plant at chernobyl. People are not allowed to live near it, even though it has been many years since the disaster.

The weather in Ukraine

In the north and west of Ukraine much more rain falls throughout the year than in the south and south-east.

Winters are very cold and there is a lot of snow.

It can snow a lot in the Carpathian Mountains, in the east of Ukraine.

Summers in Ukraine are warm. It is very hot in the south so lots of people go on holiday to the Black Sea coast.

Ukraine's coast is on the Black Sea, where lots of people go to swim.

I like to go to the beach and swim in the sea.

9

People who live in Ukraine

Ukraine's **ancestors** have come from all over the world.

Many people in Ukraine come from other European countries, such as Russia and Turkey.

Ukraine was once part of Russia and so a lot of people speak both Ukrainian and Russian.

Religious buildings are beautifully decorated. Religion is very important in Ukraine and most people are Christians. You can see churches in most towns.

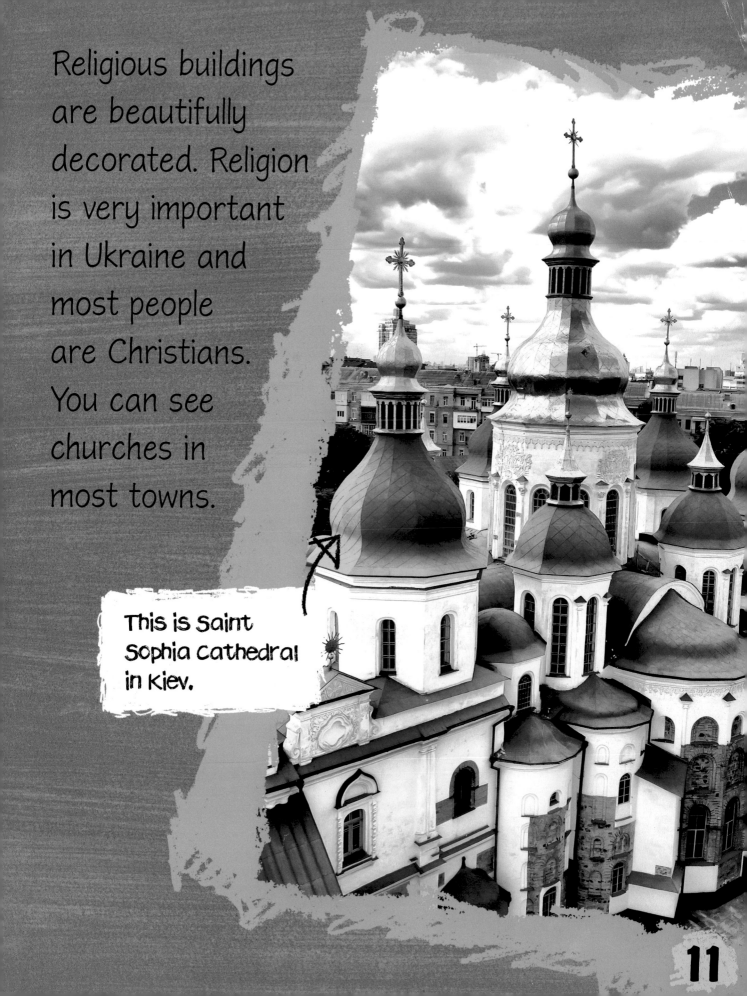

This is Saint Sophia Cathedral in Kiev.

At home with my family

I live with my mum, dad, grandmother and my big brother, Aleksandr. We call our grandmother 'Baba'.

Families are very important to people in Ukraine.

Like my family, in Ukraine many **generations** live together.

Our family has a house in the city and also a house in the countryside, called a dacha.

It has a big garden and we grow fruit and vegetables.

Many families have a second home in the countryside.

Our dacha is lots of fun in the summer. I like to help in the garden.

What we eat

Borscht is a soup made from vegetables, including beetroot.

History has taught people in Ukraine how important food is. There were once terrible **famines** across the country.

We eat lots of soups and stews made with vegetables and herbs. The most famous is *borscht*.

Another of the national foods is *salo*, which is **cured** pork fat.

People like to eat *salo* with bread as a snack.

Mum is very proud of her cooking and likes to invite people over for dinner.

People love to eat together and share food and drink tea.

Going to school

I am at an elementary school. This is the school for children aged six to ten. My brother, Aleksandr, is in the lower secondary school, which has children from ten to 15.

All children attend school until they are 15.

School is fun! When I grow up I want to be a pilot.

When Aleksandr leaves school he can choose to go to an upper secondary or a vocational school.

The vocational school will teach him to do a particular job.

young people study at upper secondary schools to go to university.

Festivals and celebrations

There are many days that we celebrate in Ukraine.

New Year's Eve is a very popular holiday. We decorate a New Year Tree and give each other presents.

Easter is an important holiday. We celebrate with lots of eating and singing.

At Easter we decorate eggs in bright colours.

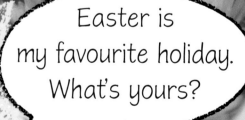

Easter is my favourite holiday. What's yours?

18

On 24 August we celebrate Independence Day. This remembers the day in 1991 when Ukraine became independent from the **Soviet Union**.

Independence Day is celebrated with parades and public performances.

Things to see

There are many exciting places to visit in Ukraine.

I like visiting the Khotyn Fortress. It was built to defend the country from enemy attacks.

The Khotyn Fortress is 1,000 years old!

My auntie is going to take us to visit the Sofiyivka Park.

This is the National **Dendrological Park,** a beautiful garden where they study plants and trees.

The National Dendrological Park has lots of special trees and places to explore.

Here are some facts about my country!

Fast facts about Ukraine

Capital city = Kiev
Population = 45,134,707
Currency = Ukraine Hryvnia (UAH)
Area = 603,550km^2
Main language = Ukrainian,
many people also speak Russian
National holiday = Independence Day, 24 August
Main religion = Ukrainian Orthodox
Longest river = Dnieper, also known as Dnipro (2,285km)
Highest mountain = Hora Hoverla (2,061m)

Glossary

ancestor a person you are related to, who lived a long time ago

cereals wheat, barley and rye

cure to salt, smoke or dry meat or fish so it will keep for a long time

contaminated to make dirty, unusable or dangerous

Dendrological Park a place where trees and shrubs are studied

famine a lack or shortage of food in a large area for a long time

fertile soil that is good for growing crops

generations layers of family that are born one after the other, such as grandparents, parents and children

nuclear power plant a place where power is created using nuclear reactions

radioactive material that gives off radioactive energy which can damage living things

Soviet Union country made up of Russia, Ukraine and other neighbouring countries

steppe a large area of flat grassland without trees

Websites

http://kids.yahoo.com/reference/world-factbook/country/up--Ukraine

Yahoo Kids! website with interesting information about Ukraine.

www.mamalisa.com/?t=ec&p=984&c=152

Songs and rhymes from Ukraine.

Books

Moving to Britain from Ukraine by Deborah Chancellor (Franklin Watts, 2008)

Index